Table of Contents

Beta Omicron Sigma
P.O. Box 272113, Columbus, OH 43227
614-845-1914
columbussigmasbos@gmail.com

President
Bro. Hiram Jones
hjonz105@gmail.com

Vice President
Bro. Derek Lee, MEd
dereklee776@gmail.com

Second Vice President
Bro. James Burke
James.burke.iv@gmail.com

Sigma Beta Club, Director
Bro. Larry Jackson
marauders2012@gmail.com

Treasurer
Bro. Joseph McKelvey, Jr.
mmckelvey@wideopenwest.com

Chaplain
Bro. Preslin Isaac
haitianpoet1985@yahoo.com

Director of Programs
Bro. Andre Harper
dreharper@gmail.com

Secretary
Bro. Michael Tyler, II
mtyler2468@gmail.com

2016 Annual Chapter Report
BETA OMICRION SIGMA CHAPTER
Columbus, OH
www.WeAreBOS.org

Written by Bro. Andre Harper
Edited by Bro. Andre Harper
Cover Design by Bro. Andre Harper
Research by Bro. Andre Harper

Contributors: The Honorable Bro. Carter D. Womack, Bro. Andre Harper, Bro. Hiram Jones,
Bro. Derek Lee, Bro. James Burke, Bro. Michael Tyler, and Bro. Joseph McKelvey

Photography: Bro. James Burke and Bro. Ulysses Ford

Printed in the United States of America

First Printing, 2017

ISBN-13: 978-1541350960 (CreateSpace-Assigned)
ISBN-10: 1541350960

Beta Omicron Sigma Alumni Chapter
P.O. Box 272113
Columbus, OH 43227
614-845-1914

www.WeAreBOS.org
Facebook: "ColumbusSigmasBOS"
Instagram: "ColumbusSigmasBOS"
Twitter: @ColumbusSigmas

Columbus, OH

The Beta Omicron Sigma Alumni Chapter of Phi Beta Sigma Fraternity, Inc. was founded on June 4, 1949 and has been an active and engaged force in the Greater Columbus community ever since.

Columbus is largest city of the state of Ohio as well as the capitol. It is the 15th largest city in the United States, with a population of 835,957 (2014 estimate). It is the core city of the Columbus, OH Metropolitan Statistical Area (MSA), which encompasses a ten county area. Under the Metropolitan Statistical Area (MSA) model, it is the third largest metropolitan area in Ohio, virtually tied with the Cleveland MSA and slightly behind the Cincinnati MSA (which includes portions of Kentucky and Indiana). Under the Combined Statistical Area (CSA) model, the Columbus, OH Metropolitan Statistical Area was the 28th largest in the United States.

The city has a diverse economy based on education, government, insurance, banking, fashion, defense, aviation, food, clothes, logistics, steel, energy, medical research, health care, hospitality, retail, and technology. Columbus is home to the Battelle Memorial Institute, the world's largest private research and development foundation; Chemical Abstracts Service, the world's largest clearinghouse of chemical information; NetJets, the world's largest fractional ownership jet aircraft fleet; and The Ohio State University, one of the largest universities in the United States. As of 2013, the city has the headquarters of five corporations in the U.S. Fortune 500: Nationwide Mutual Insurance Company, American Electric Power, L Brands, Big Lots and Cardinal Health. The fast-food corporations Wendy's and White Castle are also based in the Columbus, Ohio metropolitan area.

In 2012, Columbus was ranked in BusinessWeek's 50 best cities in America. In 2013, Forbes gave Columbus an A rating as one of the top cities for business in the U.S., and later that year included the city on its list of Best Places for Business and Careers. Columbus was also ranked as the no. 1 up-and-coming tech city in the nation by Forbes in 2008, and the city was ranked a top ten city by Relocate America in 2010. In 2007, fDi Magazine ranked the city no. 3 in the U.S. for cities of the future, and the Columbus Zoo and Aquarium was rated no. 1 in 2009 by USA Travel Guide.

President's Message

Greetings from Beta Omicron Sigma (BOS) Chapter! Since its founding in 1949, BOS has been a positive and visible force in the community. The chapter is composed of a diverse and talented group of educated professionals who lend their skills, time, and connections to exemplifying the high ideas of Phi Beta Sigma Fraternity, Inc.

The BOS Executive Board and Chapter members accepted multiple challenges towards improving our branding and strengthening our Chapter. We first looked inside to our current membership a starting place as membership as is the backbone of any organization. We wanted to improve the engagement and bonding between our members while also improving the utilization of the talents residing within an Alumni Chapter. Additional standards were adopted to facilitate consistency, understanding, and sustainable improvements in the Chapter's business operations. We developed strategies to conduct social activities and to provide more educational programing to support the health and financial wellbeing of our members. Increasing the value proposition for members supports retention and serves as another incentive when recruiting new members. Growing our membership in turn enables the Chapter to provide more service to the community.

The Executive Board successfully executed a strategy to raise both our presence and brand by doing a better job of sharing the good news and results of our service to the community. We modernized our communications and networking approach to take full advantage of the media, web, social applications, corporate sponsors, and relationship with other Greek organizations to increase awareness of our activities and the impact that we can obtain. Events such as Our Clothing Drive and Sigma Bazaar, Blue Salute to Veterans and Sigma Santa, have been featured during local news and radio broadcast. The Chapter is sought after and recognized as an action oriented organization that provides real value to the community.

We demonstrated our concern and commitment in supporting our young men by successfully chartering our Sigma Beta Club. We have been focused on executing the Rise and Thunder curriculum as well as increasing mentorship, scholastic support, and mentoring opportunities. BOS has a strong relationship with two local chapters of Zeta Phi Beta Sorority, Inc. All three chapters support one and another's programs and activities. The president of each chapter meets quarterly to share insights, calendars, plans, and to identify assistance that is needed to support collegiate chapters and the youth within the greater Columbus area.

It is my pleasure to serve as the BOS President and it is with pride that we showcase our 2016 accomplishments.

Sincerely,

Bro. Hiram Jones
President, Beta Omicron Sigma Chapter

Vice President's Message

President Barack Obama, our nation's first African-American elected president, commented to the nation, "Change will not come if we wait for some other person, or some other time. We are the ones that we've been waiting for. We are the change that we seek." As 2016 has ended, the men of Phi Beta Sigma Fraternity, Inc. Beta Omicron Sigma Chapter can comfortably say that they have embraced the concept of change, and became an active and vital force in the Greater Columbus community. The chapter realizes that the state and current condition of the African-American male will not fix itself without the efforts, skills, and talents of the men connected with this great fraternity.

Our 2016 report highlights the very concept of change: change in how we connect as brothers, change in how we connect with our community, and change in how we display our beacon of light that is Phi Beta Sigma Fraternity, Inc. Through effective service programming such as *The Sigma Bazaar*, and fundraising efforts such as *For The Lover In You,* the Beta Omicron Sigma Chapter of Phi Beta Sigma Fraternity, Inc. has been able to foster healthy relationships with community partners, as well as forward the vision of the International President of "being my brother's keeper."

"Culture for service, and service for humanity" continues to be very reason of existence for Sigma men in the Greater Columbus area. We passionately seek opportunities to be a service to all mankind, never diverting our focus off of men of color, the family unit, and the community at large!

With God's Love,

Bro. Derek D. Lee, M.Ed.
First Vice President, Beta Omicron Sigma Chapter

2016 Standards Self-Assessment Tool

Name of Chapter: Beta Omicron Sigma
City/Community: Columbus, Ohio
Chapter Address: P.O. Box 272113, Columbus, OH 43227
Chapter President: Bro. Hiram Jones
Telephone: 614-845-1914
Email: columbussigmasbos@gmail.com

Chapter Level Status: Level I

Level I Classification – Chapters with active membership with 40 or more.
Level II Classification – Chapters with active membership with 15 to 39
Level III Classification – Chapters with active membership with 5 to 14

Areas of Focus	Total Possible Score	Your chapter Points
MEMBERSHIP GROWTH AND RETENTION	90	40
CHAPTER OPERATIONS	250	235
RISK MANAGEMENT	150	150
SCHOLARSHIP AND ACADEMIC ACHIEVEMENT	100	100
PROGRAM IMPLEMENTATION AND REPORTING	300	295
BONUS POINTS		70
Total	890	890

Chapter Overall Performance Levels and Analysis	Check One
If your chapter score is 741-915+, your chapter is rated Gold Status	X
If your chapter score is 641-740, your chapter is rated Silver Status	
If your chapter score is 541-640, your chapter is rated Bronze Status	
If your chapter score is below 541, your chapter is rated Marginal Status	

Chapters in Marginal Status will be placed on performance review until performance is brought up to a minimum of Bronze Status

-All Reports Will Be Submitted Electronically-

Prior to Submitting, chapter will confirm that all information in report is presented accurate and true. Any falsification of in this report will result in chapter suspension. Each Regional Director will review and approve his chapters' report and forward to Corporate Headquarters for processing. Any chapter that does not submit report to Regional Director during required period will be suspended.

Scholarship and Academic Achievement

BOS is a very academically and professionally accomplished chapter. We are also vibrant and demographically diverse. We conducted a survey to get a glimpse of our chapter composition. Here are some of the results:

- 100% of our members have completed undergraduate degrees and 32% of our members completed graduate degrees. We are also evenly spread among ages groups.
- Our chapter has a healthy mix of age groups with the largest group being the 21 to 30 age group: 65 to 75 (13%), 55 to 64 (17%), 45 to 54 (25%), 31 to 44 (17%) and 21 to 30 (29%)
- We have a wide range of professions in our chapter with Business and Financial Operations Occupations (13%), Computer and Mathematical Occupations (13%), Community and Social Service Occupations (13%) Architecture and Engineering Occupations (9%), and Management Occupations (9%) taking the largest share.
- Most our members (55%) have been financial for the last 1-5 years, 14% have for 5-10 years, 9% for 10 plus years and we proudly boast 5 life members.
- 39% are either retired, Presently Active Duty or Active Reserve or honorably discharged veterans.
- 41% of our members are married.
- 58% of our members joined the fraternity as undergraduates.
- 17% of our members are retired.

Surveymonkey.com chapter survey- December 2016

BOS brothers at the 2016 For The Lover In You

Delta Omicron Chapter
The Ohio State University

Beta Omicron Sigma advises the Delta Omicron Chapter at The Ohio State University (DO). The 2015-2016 was another phenomenal year for the chapter. They have maintained their place as one of the top Greek-letter organizations at the university by continuing to maintain high GPAs, stellar programing, having members that are engaged in campus leadership and above all else, member are graduating on time.

In 2015 the chapter brought in a total of 8 new members. Those members included Alante' Ward, Michael Golden, Kellen Milton, Dexter Haynes, Louis Halley, Surafel Ejigu, Jamahl Jones, and Cin'Quan Haney. In the spring of 2016 four new brothers joined they were Darien Dumetz, Brandon Boatner, Zachery Burton, and Frederick Ponder. At end of the 2015-2016 school year the chapter had a total of 13 brothers.

Names of 2015-present Graduates and Majors:
- Michael Golden- Public Affairs
- Kellen Milton- Corporate Finance
- Surafel Ejigu-Psychology
- Dexter Haynes- Construction Systems Management

Awards of 2015-Fall 2016
- Chapter of the Year
- Highest GPA
- Stroll Competition first runner-up
- Stroll Competition Champions
- Outstanding Scholarship Program
- Outstanding Recruitment-Intake Program
- Outstanding Senior
- Outstanding Member Development
- NPHC Advisor of the year (Derek Lee)

Project S.E.E.D.
Sigma Economic Empowerment Development Project
Chapter Programming

Date: 4/9/16

Venue/Activity Location: Columbus South High School
Area of Focus: Bigger & Better Business

Description of Activity/Program: The Sigma Economic Empowerment Development Project (Project SEED) is a Bigger & Better Business program developed to focus on two important topics of interest: Financial Management and Home Ownership. This focus provides useful information in both areas and benefits Phi Beta Sigma members, families, and communities. Project SEED is designed to be implemented at all organizational levels, by alumni and collegiate chapters. Each of the program's components are economically viable and relevant, current concerns of our membership.

Program Director: Bro. Andre Harper
Committee Members: Bro. C. Hill, Bro. J. McKelvey, Bro. E. Locklear, Bro. C. Marsh, Bro. C. Hopkins, Bro. M. Tyler

What were the intended goals of the program/activity? Soror Tasha Macklin spoke about on Financial and Estate Planning.

Type of Media Coverage: Social Media

Program Implementation and Reporting

Executive Summary: 2016 was another banner year for BOS. The administration set a goal of making BOS a leading chapter among the entire fraternity. To do that, we had to revamp our programming and philanthropic endeavors. It started at the end of 2015 at our executive retreat. There we developed an annual calendar with a mixture of events designed to maximize effectiveness, reach and participation. A major consideration was to become a "mainstream" entity in Columbus by conducting events that appeal outside of our traditional constituencies.

We maintained our gold chapter status as one of the highest performing chapters by scoring 890/890 possible points based on the fraternity's scoring model (*total includes bonus points.*)

Our service hours, reach, community engagement, philanthropy, membership engagement and chapter revenue has seen a seismic shift. Formerly inactive brothers are coming back, community organizations are contacting us to participate in their activities and new men are expressing interest in joining our wondrous band.

In 2017, we look to build upon the gains of 2016 and strive to increase our membership and community engagement.

Sincerely,

Bro. Andre Harper
Program Director

Program Director: Bro. Andre Harper
Committee Members: Bro. C. Hill, Bro. J. McKelvey, Bro. E. Locklear, Bro. C. Marsh, Bro. C. Hopkins, Bro. M. Tyler
Total of service hours*: 1232
Total of people served*: 6566

Community Partners: Zeta Phi Beta Sorority Inc. (Sigma Iota Zeta Chapter, Gamma Zeta Zeta Chapter & Xi Gamma Chapter, Delta Omicron Chapter (Phi Beta Sigma), Barnett Recreation Center, Buckeye Crazy Sports Bar, Barnett Recreation Center Civic Association, Columbus South High School, Tuskegee Airmen Inc. (Ohio Memorial Chapter), King Art Complex, Grange Friendly Hills Campsite (Zanesville, Ohio), The African American Male Wellness Walk Initiative, Academy of Ophthalmology, Chi Eta Phi Sorority Incorporated, The Ohio Commission on Minority Health, The National Youth Sports Health & Safety Institute, The Ohio Foot and Medical Association and the Columbus Police Department Leadership At Its Best, Barnett Recreation Civic Association, Columbus Parks & Recreation, the A. Philip Randolph Institute and Redeemed Christian Church of God.

Summary of Local Programs: BOS focused on creating indigenous events that focus on the needs of our local community in addition to our fraternity mandated activities. This approach led us to the development of well supported programs and increased our local reach.

List Local Programs: Sigma Supper Club, The Blue Salute, Breakfast with Sigma Santa, Sigma Santa Networking Social/Toy Drive, Brotherhood Night, Sigma Bazaar/Clothing Drive

List of Fraternity Programs: Sigma Wellness: Living Well Brother-to-Brother, March-of-Dimes, VITA, Adopt-A-School, Project Vote

Fundraising

To continue BOS's effective programming and philanthropic traditions, we maintained our fundraising strategy to maximize profits and participation among the community we serve as well as the brotherhood. This is done by maintaining our established portfolio of minimum, medium and major fundraisers. These events are strategically planned over the course of the year to complement other chapter activities as well as to be aware of events planned by other organizations.

Our signature events included *Lover In You*, *The Second Hand Jam* and *The Blue Salute*. All events were profitable and provided memorable experiences for all in attendance.

Philanthropy

BOS prides itself on continuously giving financial as well as in-kind gifts to the people we serve. We have made it to give generously above our fraternity mandated donations to the March of Dimes. In 2016, BOS gave over $5000 in philanthropic donations. This includes free breakfast and toys to over 300 guests at *Breakfast with Sigma Santa*, collected and distributed over 100 filled book bags to local elementary schools, over 80 free breakfasts to veterans at *The Blue Salute* and Easter gift cards and donations to children at the Barnett Recreation Center for the annual Easter Egg Hunt. We also provided over $1000 in scholarships, transportation and donations to Sigma Beta Club members attending local colleges as well as Lincoln University of Missouri.

***Based on Blueprint Submission**

BOS and Zetas present a $300 donation to the Barnett Recreation Center

Family Clothing Drive
Social Action

Date: March 2016 – April 2016

Venue/Activity Location: Barnett Recreation Center

Area of Focus: Social Action

Description of Activity/Program: Each spring, BOS collects clothing for 2 months to be given away at our annual Sigma Bazaar. Members collect clothes from neighbors, co-workers, family and friends. The columbus community has been very supportive of the program. In 2016, our community partner, Grandma' Closet Thrift Store, donated their entire store's remaining inventory after the store closed down.

Program Director: Bro. Andre Harper
Committee Members: Bro. C. Hill, Bro. J. McKelvey, Bro. E. Locklear, Bro. C. Marsh, Bro. C. Hopkins, Bro. M. Tyler

What were the intended goals of the program/activity?

Number of Service Hours: 40

Community Partners: Barnett Recreation Center, NPHC, Grandma' Closet Thrift Store

Type of Media Coverage: Phi Beta Sigma Weekly News, Social Media

Sigma Bazaar
Social Action

Date: 4/30/16

Venue/Activity Location: Barnett Recreation Center
Area of Focus: Social Action

Description of Activity/Program: BOS hosted the Sigma Bazaar where Columbus area families were welcome to get clothing free of charge. We created a welcoming environment with music and brothers assisting with gathering and transporting to vehicles. Guests were encourgaged to bring bags. The remaining clothes were donated to Redeemed Christian Church of God. These items were used to help foreign religious missions.

Program Director: Bro. Andre Harper
Committee Members: Bro. C. Hill, Bro. J. McKelvey, Bro. E. Locklear, Bro. C. Marsh, Bro. C. Hopkins, Bro. M. Tyler

What were the intended goals of the program/activity? Over 200 guests could get clothing free of charge at the Sigma Bazaar.

Number of Service Hours: 250
Number of people served? 250
Community Partners: Barnett Recreation Center & Redeemed Christian Church of God American

Type of Media Coverage: Phi Beta Sigma Weekly News, Social Media

Community Health Fair
Social Action

Date: 4/30/16

Venue/Activity Location: Barnett Recreation Center
Area of Focus: Living Well Brother to Brother

Description of Activity/Program: BOS is excited about Sigma's leadership role in eliminating health disparities in men of color. Local healthcare professionals gave for screenings and preventative care education. Health care professionals presented information from our health care modules are their various stations and in the presentation area.

Program Director: Bro. Andre Harper
Committee Members: Bro. C. Hill, Bro. J. McKelvey, Bro. E. Locklear, Bro. C. Marsh, Bro. C. Hopkins, Bro. M. Tyler

What were the intended goals of the program/activity? Local healthcare professionals provided screenings and preventative care education. The Health Fair is sponsored by the American Academy of Ophthalmology, Chi Eta Phi Sorority Incorporated, The Ohio Commission on Minority Health, The National Youth Sports Health & Safety Institute, The Ohio Foot and Medical Association and the Columbus Police Department. Over 250 guests had access to free health screenings and to attend Living Well Brother to Brother sessions lead by local health professionals.

Number of Service Hours: 50
Number of people served? 250
Living Well Brother to Brother Modules Completed: Module-1: Living Health Diet And Nutrition, Module-2: Living Fit Obesity Weight Control, Module-3: Reducing Your Cancer Risk & Module-5: Living Balanced Spiritual Mental Health

Community Partners: Barnett Recreation Center, Academy of Ophthalmology, Chi Eta Phi Sorority Incorporated, The Ohio Commission on Minority Health, The National Youth Sports Health & Safety Institute, The Ohio Foot and Medical Association and the Columbus Police Department
Type of Media Coverage: Phi Beta Sigma Weekly News, Social Media

The 2ⁿᵈ Hand Jam
Social Action

Date: 4/30/16

Venue/Activity Location: The Venice Club
Area of Focus: Social Action

Description of Activity/Program: In conjunction with our annual Sigma Bazaar family clothing giveaway, the men of the Beta Omicron Sigma Chapter of Phi Beta Sigma Fraternity, Inc. held a night of fun and eclectic fashion. Supporters dressed to impress with their favorite thrift shop inspired attire. Participants enjoyed an evening of style, music and dinner. Cash prizes were awarded to the most eclectic outfits. Ticket included open bar and dinner. All proceeds went to March of Dimes and community empowerment initiatives.

Program Director: Bro. Andre Harper
Committee Members: Bro. C. Hill, Bro. J. McKelvey, Bro. E. Locklear, Bro. C. Marsh, Bro. C. Hopkins, Bro. M. Tyler

What were the intended goals of the program/activity? The goal of the event was to bring awareness to our annual Sigma Bazaar and Health Fair. It was the final event of our Spring Service Weekend. Our creative campaign promoting the event increased our social media presence including public pages on Facebook, Instagram and Twitter tremendously. The campaign highlighted some of the most revered Black musical artists. It resulted in over 12,000 views over the final month leading up to the event.

Community Partners: March of Dimes
Type of Media Coverage: Social Media

National Gun Violence Awareness March
Social Action

Date: 6/2/16

Venue/Activity Location: Downtown Columbus
Area of Focus: Social Action

Description of Activity/Program: BOS participated in the The National Gun Violence Awareness Day Event: National Gun Violence Awareness Day (Wear Orange Day). It was created with the goal of pulling the community together to take a unified stand against gun violence. Radio Operations Manager (BOS Chapter Brother) Big Bink Turner of Power 107.5, and community leaders organized the march in response to the recent rise of gun violence in the community and discussed how we can come together to put an end to it. Attendees are asked to wear orange.

Program Director: Bro. Andre Harper
Committee Members: Bro. C. Hill, Bro. J. McKelvey, Bro. E. Locklear, Bro. C. Marsh, Bro. C. Hopkins, Bro. M. Tyler

What were the intended goals of the program/activity? Members of BOS continue to be active in the Columbus community by engaging in leadership meetings as well as public gatherings to maintain our brand.

Number of Service Hours: 12
Number of people served? 500
Community Partners: Radio One Public Affairs Director/ Joy 107.1 Mid-Day host Yaves Ellis, Misty Jordan of Magic 95.5, Radio Operations Manager (BOS Chapter Brother) Big Bink Turner of Power 107.5, City News of Boom 106.3, Mayor Andrew Ginther, Radio One Columbus, Columbus Parks and Recreations
Type of Media Coverage: Social Media

MLK Commemorative March
Social Action

Date: 1/18/16

Venue/Activity Location: King Art Complex
Area of Focus: Social Action

Description of Activity/Program: BOS participated in the annual MLK Weekend March. The theme was "Faith is taking the first step, even when you don't see the whole staircase."

Program Director: Bro. Andre Harper
Committee Members: Bro. C. Hill, Bro. J. McKelvey, Bro. E. Locklear, Bro. C. Marsh, Bro. C. Hopkins, Bro. M. Tyler

What were the intended goals of the program/activity? Members of BOS continue to be active in the Columbus community by engaging in leadership meetings as well as public gatherings to maintain our brand.

Number of Service Hours: 34
Number of people served: 500
Community Partners: King Arts Complex
Type of Media Coverage: Social Media

March of Dimes Walk
Social Action

Date: 5/1/2016

Venue/Activity Location: COSI, Columbus, (Center of Science and Industry)
Area of Focus: Social Action

Description of Activity/Program: Phi Beta Sigma partners with the March of Dimes. Through this partnership, the two organizations will work together to prevent premature births and build strong fathers and male role models in the African American community through sponsoring Strong Fathers seminars and Stepping To Save Babies.

Program Director: Bro. Hiram Jones
Committee Members: Entire chapter

What were the intended goals of the program/activity? BOS raised $1100, exceeding our chapter goal of $1000. We were joined at the walk by our Sigma Beta Club members, Sorors of Zeta Phi Beta Sorority, Inc., in addition to over 20 chapter members.

Number of Service Hours: 60

Community Partners: March of Dimes, Zeta Phi Beta Sorority, Inc.
Type of Media Coverage: Social Media

Barnett Recreation Center Easter Egg Hunt Drive
Social Action

Date: 3/26/2016

Venue/Activity Location: Barnett Recreation Center
Area of Focus: Social Action

Description of Activity/Program: BOS donated over $250 in Easter egg hunt supplies including baskets, candy and empty plastic eggs for the center's annual youth egg hunt. We also donated a $100 Target Gift card for additional supplies.

Program Director: Bro. Andre Harper
Committee Members: Bro. C. Hill, Bro. J. McKelvey, Bro. E. Locklear, Bro. C. Marsh, Bro. C. Hopkins, Bro. M. Tyler

What were the intended goals of the program/activity? BOS has a great relationship with the Barnett Recreation center. The director, Ms. Theresa Featherstone, knows that she can contact BOS and we will be there to help. She says that we are the only civic organizations that continues to make an ongoing presence in the Columbus East community and continually reaches out to them for support. We want to continue to grow our relationship with them.

Number of Service Hours: 10
Number of people served? 200
Community Partners: Barnett Recreation Center
Type of Media Coverage: Social Media

Breaking the Blues Stigma
Social Action

Date: 5/21/2016

Venue/Activity Location: Dodge Recreational Park

Area of Focus: Social Action

Description of Activity/Program: Title sponsors for "Breaking the Blues Stigma," hosted by Gamma Zeta Zeta chapter of Zeta Phi Beta Sorority, Inc.

Program Director: Bro. Michael Tyler
Committee Members: Bro. C. Hill, Bro. J. McKelvey, Bro. C. Womack, Bro. C. J. Copeland, Bro. C. Hopkins

What were the intended goals of the program/activity? As the title sponsor, we were allotted time to discuss portions of our Living Well Brother-to-Brother initiative, specifically about black men and the stigmas behind mental health awareness.

Number of Service Hours: 6
Number of people served? 20
Community Partners: Gamma Zeta Zeta chapter of Zeta Phi Beta Sorority, Inc.
Type of Media Coverage: Social Media

The National African American Male Wellness Walk
Social Action

Date: 8/13/ 2016

Venue/Activity Location: Livingston Park, Columbus OH
Area of Focus: Social Action

Description of Activity/Program: The annual African American Male Wellness Walk Celebrates health & wellness with screenings, Education, Exercise And FUN! 20 Men of BOS participated in the 3 mile walk and 2 brothers ran in the 5 mile run. All brothers paticiatpated in health screenings including blood pressure, blood, body mass and HIV. The Sigma Beta Club also participated in the walk.

Program Director: Bro. Andre Harper
Committee Members: Bro. C. Hill, Bro. J. McKelvey, Bro. E. Locklear, Bro. C. Marsh, Bro. C. Hopkins, Bro. M. Tyler

What were the intended goals of the program/activity? Over 2000 people enjoyed live entertainment, free health screenings, a 5K walk/run, job fair and free immunizations.

Number of Service Hours: 60
Number of people served: 2000
Community Partners: The African American Male Wellness Walk Initiative

Type of Media Coverage: Social Media

Project Vote
Social Action

Date: 11/3/2016

Venue/Activity Location: A. Philip Randolph Institute Columbus Office
Area of Focus: Social Action

Description of Activity/Program: The brothers of BOS helped to call over 2000 homes to encourage and confirm that they will be voting in the 2016 election. Brothers also volunteer on election day at several high-risk precincts as part of APRI's election protection to ensure that there were not irregularities. The A. Phillip Randolph Institute (APRI) is a labor rights organization founded in 1965 by labor union pioneer Bro. A. Philip Randolph and civil rights activist Bayard Rustin. APRI is currently led by President Clayola Brown, who began serving as the national president of A. Philip Randolph Institute, located in Washington, D.C., in August 2004.

Program Director: Bro. Andre Harper
Committee Members: Bro. C. Hill, Bro. J. McKelvey, Bro. E. Locklear, Bro. C. Marsh, Bro. C. Hopkins, Bro. M. Tyler

What were the intended goals of the program/activity? The men of BOS took an active part in the crucial election of 2016. We phone banked, poll watched and registered voters.

Number of Service Hours: 12
Number of people served: 300
Community Partners: Zeta Phi Beta Sorority, Inc. & the A. Philip Randolph Institute

Type of Media Coverage: Social Media

The Blue Salute
Social Action

Date: 11/12/2016

Venue/Activity Location: Columbus South High School
Area of Focus: Social Action

Description of Activity/Program: BOS honored veterans by hosting a pancake breakfast. The breakfast featured pancakes, bacon, sausage, eggs and fruit. The title sponsor of our event was Thompson, Steward Fletch, LLC, Attorneys & Counselors At Law. Our featured speaker was Bro. Jeff Watkins. LTC Watkins serves as Commander of the 52nd Civil Support Team (WMD), National Guard of the Ohio Adjutant General Department. LTC Watkins has served in the National Guard for over 30 years.

Program Director: Bro. J. McKelvey
Committee Members: Bro. C. Hill, Bro. A. Harper, Bro. E. Locklear, Bro. C. Marsh, Bro. C. Hopkins, Bro. M. Tyler

What were the intended goals of the program/activity? The goal was intended to honor veterans and continue build our reputation in Columbus, as a mainstream service organization.

Number of Service Hours: 105
Number of people served? 60
Community Partners: Thompson, Steward Fletch, LLC, Attorneys & Counselors At Law and Columbus South High School

Type of Media Coverage: social media

Adopt-A-School
Education

Date: 9/7/2016

Venue/Activity Location: South High School
Area of Focus: Education

Description of Activity/Program: Clumbus South High School is the the focus of our Adopt-A-School efforts. We have maintained presence at the school for years. We held our 11th Annual Blue & White School Supply Drive. Beta Omicron Sigma, along with Zeta Phi Beta Sorority, Inc.-Sigma Iota Zeta Chapter, Reynoldsburg, OH and Zeta Phi Beta Sorority, Inc., Gamma Zeta Zeta Chapter (Columbus, Ohio), collected school supplies to help elementary schools located in the south side of Columbus.

Program Director: Bro. Michael Tyler
Committee Members: Hon. Bro. Carter D. Womack, Bro. Mike Owens, Bro. Joseph McKelvey, Br. Joseph Copeland and Bro. John Whitten

What were the intended goals of the program/activity? We donated 4 bins filled with school supplies and a check for $300 for additional supplies to be distributed to several schools on Columbus's south side which were distributed to in-need students in the schools.
Community Partners: Zeta Phi Beta Sorority, Inc.

Type of Media Coverage: Social Media

BOS Scholarship Presentation
Education

Date: 7/25/16

Venue/Activity Location: South High School
Area of Focus: Education
Description of Activity/Program: The Beta Omicron Sigma Chapter presented a $1000 to David Via as part of the chapter's African American Male Leadership Program Scholarship.

Program Director: Bro. Joseph McKelvey

Committee Members: Hon. Bro. Carter D. Womack, Bro. Mike Owens, Bro. Joseph McKelvey, Br. Joseph Copeland and Bro. John Whitten

What were the intended goals of the program/activity? The goal of the program is to offer mentoring and scholarships to African-American males.

Community Partners: Leadership At Its Best

Type of Media Coverage: Social Media

The Blue Debut: Breaking Blue
Bigger & Better Business

Date: 2/29/16

Venue/Activity Location: Buckeye Crazy

Area of Focus: Bigger & Better Business (Project SEED)

Description of Activity/Program: The men of the BOS hosted The Blue Debut: Breaking Blue at Buckeye Crazy Sports Bar. It is a black-owned business that we promoted as part of Project SEED. We welcomed over 70 family and friends to The Blue Debut: Breaking Blue! We introduced the newest members, Bro. Kabimbi Kalubi and Bro. Will Damson, of our great Fraternity and the Columbus Pan-Hellenic Community. This was a joint endaeavor to promote the a local black business.

Program Director: Bro. Andre Harper
Committee Members: Bro. C. Hill, Bro. J. McKelvey, Bro. E. Locklear, Bro. C. Marsh, Bro. C. Hopkins, Bro. M. Tyler

What were the intended goals of the program/activity? The goal of the event was to promote a local black business, Buckeye Crazy Sports Bar by publicly introduce our newest fraternity to the community.

Number of Service Hours: 75
Number of people served? 60
Community Partners: Buckeye Crazy Sports Bar
Type of Media Coverage: Social Media

Bigger And Better Business
Bigger & Better Business

Date: 9/3/2016

Venue/Activity Location: Buckeye Crazy Restaurant & Sports Bar
Area of Focus: Bigger And Better Business

Description of Activity/Program: The men of BOS encouraged friends to meet at Buckeye Crazy for the Ohio State University football season opener. We celebrate black owned business as part of our Fraternity's Project SEED. The Sigma Economic Empowerment Development Project (Project SEED) is a Bigger & Better Business initiative.

Pan-Hellenic Council Representative:
Committee Members:

What were the intended goals of the program/activity This activity was to showcase some of the amazing Black owned businesses in Columbus as well as show off the amazing food and atmosphere of one of the area's great sports bars.

Number of Service Hours: 24
Number of people served: 8

The Blue Debut: T.U.R.M.O.I.L.E.D Trilogy
Bigger & Better Business

Date: 12/6/16

Venue/Activity Location: Buckeye Crazy Sports Bar
Area of Focus: Bigger & Better Business (Project SEED)

Description of Activity/Program: The men of the BOS hosted this event at Buckeye Crazy Sports Bar, a minority-owned business as part of Project SEED. We welcomed over 70 family and friends to The Blue Debut: T.U.R.M.O.I.L.E.D Trilogy! We introduced the newest members, Bro. James Smith, Bro. Micheal Henderson and Bro. Robert Miller, of our great Fraternity and the Columbus Pan-Hellenic Community. This was a joint endeavor to promote the a local black business.

Program Director: Bro. Andre Harper
Committee Members: Bro. C. Hill, Bro. J. McKelvey, Bro. E. Locklear, Bro. C. Marsh, Bro. C. Hopkins, Bro. M. Tyler, Bro. W. Damson, Bro. D. Lee, Bro. M. Tyler

What were the intended goals of the program/activity? The goal of the event was to promote a local black business, Buckeye Crazy Sports Bar by publicly introduce our newest fraternity to the community.

Number of Service Hours: 75
Number of people served? 60
Community Partners: Buckeye Crazy Sports Bar
Type of Media Coverage: Social Media

Sigma Santa Networking Social/Toy Drive
Bigger & Better Business

Date: 12/17/16

Venue/Activity Location: Buckeye Crazy Sports Bar
Area of Focus: Bigger & Better Business (Project S.E.E.D.)

Description of Activity/Program: Columbus Area chapters of Zeta Phi Beta Sorority, Inc. and Phi Beta Sigma Fraternity, Inc. hosted our our annual Sigma Santa Networking Social at Buckeye Crazy Sports Bar, a minority-owned business as part of Project S.E.E.D. The five chapters collected over 400 toys that were donated at the Breakfast with Sigma Santa event.

Program Director: Bro. Andre Harper
Committee Members: Bro. C. Womack, Bro. C. Hill, Bro. J. McKelvey, Bro. J. Merriweather, Bro. C. Hopkins, Bro. D. Lee, Bro. A. Ward, Bro. J. Burke

What were the intended goals of the program/activity? We collected over 150 new unwrapped toys.

Number of Service Hours: 30
Number of people served? 50

Community Partners: Buckeye Crazy Sports Bar, Barnett Recreation Center, Barnett Recreation Civic Association, Columbus Parks & Recreation, Sigma Iota Zeta (Zeta Phi Beta), Gamma Zeta Zeta (Zeta Phi Beta) Xi Gamma (Zeta Phi Beta) & Delta Omicron (Phi Beta Sigma)
Type of Media Coverage: Social Media

Breakfast With Sigma Santa
Volunteer Income Tax Assistance (VITA)
Chapter Programming

Date: 12/17/16

Venue/Activity Location: Barnett Recreation Center
Area of Focus: Bigger & Better Business (VITA)

Description of Activity/Program: The Columbus, OH Area chapters of Zeta Phi Beta Sorority, Inc. (3) and Phi Beta Sigma Fraternity, Inc. (2) held their annual Breakfast with Sigma Santa which provided nearly 300 kids with toys as well as providing breakfast to over 150 parents and volunteers. They presented the Barnett Recreation Center a $300 check for center programs. Kids got their pictures taken with Sigma Santa and parents were got information about free tax preparation through our Volunteer Income Tax Assistance (VITA) from volunteer financial advisers. Parents were also able to meet with representatives from Federal Express were on hand to hire new employees. We adopted a family whose father recently passed. We gave several toys to his kids and grandkids family.

Program Director: Bro. Andre Harper

Committee Members: Bro. C. Womack, Bro. C. Hill, Bro. J. McKelvey, Bro. J. Merriweather, Bro. C. Hopkins, Bro. D. Lee, Bro. A. Ward, Bro. J. Burke

What were the intended goals of the program/activity? We have continued to maintain our presence in the community. We are continuing to establish a tradition of children celebrating the holidays with "Sigma Santa." We provided parents information about free tax preparation, hiring opportunities at FedEx as well as provided hot meal for them and their kids.

Number of Service Hours: 105
Number of people served? 450

Community Partners: Barnett Recreation Center
Type of Media Coverage: Social Media

2016 Annual Chapter Report
BETA OMICRION SIGMA CHAPTER
Columbus, OH
www.WeAreBOS.org

Membership Growth and Retention

2016 was a great year for member participation despite returning to "normal" levels after our fraternity centennial in 2014. However, that is no longer acceptable. We have implemented a Retention Policy focused on retention, recruitment and reclamation. Members were energized by the amount of new programming designed to increase membership and community engagement.

The biggest change was a targeted effort to increase membership with activities designed to appeal to members with varying ages and interests to reflect our diverse chapter. These activities included:

- **Brotherhood Events**- Brotherhood events included going to Sports Bars, bowling and watching football games. These events were designed to appeal to the broadest range of the members.
- **Sigma Supper Club**- the Sigma Supper Club is designed to reach out to our members who would like to meet and dine every three months at restaurants that offer different culinary experiences. Restaurants visited: Cooper Hawks Winery and Restaurant and The Hollywood Casino Epic Buffet.
- **BOS NFL Fantasy Football League**- 16 BOS and fellow Greeks were involved in the inaugural the season.
- **Sigma Signing Day**- A formal ceremony was initiated to transfer collegiate members from The Ohio State University to Beta Omicron Sigma. Collegiate brothers were presented certificates and proclamations declaring their intent to join the alumni chapter.

Submitted By: Bro. Andre Harper, Director of Programming

In 2017, we have more aggressive membership goals. We intend increase our membership to 100 through combination of intake, reclamation and college graduates.

Honorable Bro. Carter D. Womack, welomes Bro. Smith, Bro. Henderson and Bro. Miller into the fraternity.

Beta Omicron Sigma
Membership Roster
2015-2016 Executive Board

President
Bro. Hiram Jones
1982, Nu Epsilon
hjonz105@gmail.com
Capital University

Vice President
Bro. Derek Lee, MEd
Fall 2003, Delta Omicron
dereklee776@gmail.com
The Ohio State University

Second Vice President
Bro. James Burke
Fall 2006, Alpha Epsilon
James.burke.iv@gmail.com
Johnson C. Smith University

**Director Of
Sigma Beta Club**
Bro. Larry Jackson
Spr 2014, Beta Omicron Sigma
marauders2012@gmail.com
Central State University

Treasurer
Bro. Joseph McKelvey, Jr.
Summer 1977, Beta Omicron Sigma
mmckelvey@wideopenwest.com
Benedict College

Chaplain
Bro. Preslin Isaac
Spring 2010, Delta Omicron
haitianpoet1985@yahoo.com
Ohio Christian University

**Director of
Programs**
Bro. Andre Harper
Spring 2003, Alpha Eta
dreharper@gmail.com
Florida A&M University

**27th & 29th
International President**
The Honorable
Bro. Carter D. Womack
Spring 1971, Gamma Epsilon
carterlaib@aol.com
Alabama A&M University

Secretary
Bro. Michael Tyler, II
Spring 2014, Beta Xi Sigma
mtyler2468@gmail.com
Wright State University

2016 Beta Omicron Sigma Brothers

Bro. James Adams
Spring 1983, Beta Omicron Sigma
jcombs704@gmail.com
University of Toledo

Bro. Joseph Copeland
Spring 1973, Epsilon Phi (Founder)
jcope1914@sbcglobal.net
Bowling Green State University

Bro. Charles "Rick" Henderson
Spring 1980, Epsilon Phi
rhender1@insight.rr.com
Bowling Green State University

Bro. Chris Hill
Fall 1987, Chi
Chrishill1914@yahoo.com
Morehouse College

Bro. Cameron Hopkins
Fall 2012, Delta Omicron
hopkins_cameron@yahoo.com
The Ohio State University

Bro. John Merriweather
Spring 1989, Chi Sigma
jmudz@aol.com
The Ohio State University

Bro. L'Nard Tufts, II
Fall 2014, Delta Omicron
ltufts2@gmail.com
The Ohio State University

Bro. Eric Locklear
Spring 2006, Delta Omicron
Elocklear@aol.com
Denison University

Bro. Mitchell L. Lewis jr
Fall 1982, Epsilon Theta
mitchell_lewis@sbcglobal.net
Western Kentucky university

Bro. James W. Mock, Sr
Fall 1989, Beta Omicron Sigma
jwm2032@yahoo.com
Franklin University

Bro. Alante Ward
Fall 2014, Delta Omicron
alanteward@gmail.com
The Ohio State University

Bro. Alan Tucker
Spr. 1997, Delta Omicron
alantucker33@gmail.com
University of Findlay

2016 Beta Omicron Sigma Initiates

Bro. William Damson
Spring 2016, Beta Omicron Sigma
william.damson@yahoo.com
Wright State University

Bro. Mike Henderson
Fall 2016, Beta Omicron Sigma
Mike.henderson1229@gmail.com
Wright State University

Bro. Robert Miller
Spring 2016, Beta Omicron Sigma
Rmiller0803@hotmail.com
Trenholm State University

Bro. James Smith
Fall 2016, Beta Omicron Sigma
smith1.james007@gmail.com
Florida A&M University

Bro. Kabimbi Kalubi
Spring 2016, Beta Omicron Sigma
kabimbik@gmail.com
University of Cincinnati

Beta Omicron Sigma
2016 Active Roster

First Name		Last Name		Email	Profession
Bro. James		Adams		JAAdams1171@gmail.com	Retired
Bro. Theries		Benn	Jr.	tbenn513@yahoo.com	Finance
Bro. Eugene		Borders	III	borders.30@gmail.com	Human Resources
Bro. James		Burke	IV	James.burke.iv@gmail.com	Finance
Bro. Myronn		Carlock		Sigmaphine1914@gmail.com	Military
Bro. Kelvin		Cole		kcole1914@yahoo.com	Corrections
Bro. Joseph		Copeland		jcope1914@sbcglobal.net	Education
Bro. Timothy		Craft		izidizi92@gmail.com	Business
Bro. William		Damson		WDAMSON90@GMAIL.COM	Military
Bro. Gearl		Diggs		gbdiggs2@aol.com	Healthcare
Bro. Kollin		Dunson		jaedun10@outlook.com	Clergy
Bro. Ulysses		Ford	III	ulyssesford25@hotmail.com	Environmental Science
Bro. Andre		Harper		dreharper@gmail.com	Information Technology
Bro. Lester		Harris	Jr.	Lesterh027@yahoo.com	Education
Bro. Charles		Henderson		rhender1@insight.rr.com	Education
Bro. Michael		Henderson		Mike.henderson1229@gmail.com	Business
Bro. Michael		Henry	II	michael.e.henryii@gmail.com	Business
Bro. Chris		Hill		Chrishill1914@yahoo.com	Human Resources
Bro. Cameron		Hopkins		hopkins_cameron@yahoo.com	Information Technology
Bro. Preslin		Isaac		haitianpoet1985@yahoo.com	Clergy
Bro. Larry		Jackson		marauders2012@gmail.com	Education
Bro. Michael		Jackson		MHJacksn@gmail.com	Business
Bro. Hiram		Jones		hjonz105@gmail.com	Logistics
Bro. Donald		Jones		dlj59@scarletmail.rutgers.edu	Business
Bro. Kabimbi		Kalubi		kabimbik@gmail.com	Engineering
Bro. Derek		Lee		dereklee776@gmail.com	Education
Bro. Mitchell		Lewis		mitchell_lewis@sbcglobal.net	Business
Bro. Eric		Locklear		Elocklear@aol.com	Logistics

Bro.	Clifford	Marsh		cliffordmarsh@hotmail.com	Accounting
Bro.	Joseph	McKelvey	Jr.	mmckelvey@wideopenwest.com	Retired
Bro.	John	Merriweather		jlmerriw@nncogannett.com	Logistics
Bro.	Robert	Miller		Rmiller0803@hotmail.com	Information Technology
Bro.	James	Mock		jmw2032@yahoo.com	Retired
Bro.	Xavier	Myers		xmyers.0354@knightnet.urbana.edu	Criminal Justice
Bro.	Michael	Owens		Glo93@aol.com	Education
Bro.	Dale	Price		daleprice10@aol.com	Information Technology
Bro.	James	Ragland		raglandjames@hotmail.com	Business
Bro.	O'Neal	Saunders		onealesq@msn.com	Legal
Bro.	Andre	Smith	Sr.	bigdre71@sbcglobal.net	Government
Bro.	James	Smith		smith1.james007@gmail.com	Information Technology
Bro.	Richard	Taylor		otnemem7@gmail.com	Information Technology
Bro.	Alan	Tucker		alantucker33@gmail.com	Finance
Bro.	L'Nard	Tufts	II	ltufts2@gmail.com	Engineering
Bro.	L'Nard	Tufts		ltufts@core.com	Retired
Bro.	Michael	Tyler	II	mtyler2468@gmail.com	Public Relations
Bro.	Alante'	Ward		alanteward@gmail.com	Finance
Bro.	Carter	Womack		carterlaib@aol.com	Business

BOS hosted statewide initiation in 2016

Membership Growth and Retention
Chapter Programming

Founders Day
Membership

Date: 1/9/16

Venue/Activity Location: Kitchen Den Bar- Easton
Area of Focus: Membership

Description of Activity/Program: Members of BOS met at KDB Easton to celebrate Founders Day. Over 50 brothers as well as our Sorors of Zeta Phi Beta Sorority, Inc. joined us to celebrate 102 years of our Wondrous Band.

Program Director: Bro. Andre Harper
Committee Members: Bro. C. Hill, Bro. J. McKelvey, Bro. E. Locklear, Bro. C. Marsh, Bro. C. Hopkins, Bro. M. Tyler

What were the intended goals of the program/activity? The goal of the event was to create another way for brothers to interact and stay engaged with chapter activity.

Community Partners: Zeta Phi Beta Sorority, Inc.
Type of Media Coverage: Social Media

Spring Sigma Supper Club
Membership

Date: 3/11/16

Venue/Activity Location: Hollywood Casino- Epic Buffet
Area of Focus: Membership

Description of Activity/Program: The Sigma Supper Club is for Sigma brothers that want to experience dining and socializing at some of the most exclusive restaurants in the area.

Program Director: Bro. Andre Harper
Committee Members: Bro. C. Hill, Bro. J. McKelvey, Bro. E. Locklear, Bro. C. Marsh, Bro. C. Hopkins, Bro. M. Tyler

What were the intended goals of the program/activity? The goal of the event was to create another way for brothers to interact and stay engaged with chapter activity.

Type of Media Coverage: Social Media

Summer Sigma Supper Club
Chapter Programming

Date: 7/29/16

Venue/Activity Location: Hollywood Casino- Epic Buffet
Area of Focus: Membership

Description of Activity/Program: The Sigma Supper Club is for Sigma brothers that want to experience dining and socializing at some of the most exclusive restaurants in the area.

Program Director: Bro. Andre Harper
Committee Members: Bro. C. Hill, Bro. J. McKelvey, Bro. E. Locklear, Bro. C. Marsh, Bro. C. Hopkins, Bro. M. Tyler

What were the intended goals of the program/activity? The goal of the event was to create another way for brothers to interact and stay engaged with chapter activity.

Type of Media Coverage: Social Media

NFL BOS Fantasy League Draft
Chapter Programming

Date: 8/28/16

Venue/Activity Location: Bro. Chris Hill's Home
Area of Focus: Membership

Description of Activity/Program: BOS hosted the inaugural BOS Fantasy football league draft. Bro. Chris Hill hosted the event at his home with food and spirits. 2016 was another thrilling season with Bro. Eugene Borders dominating the regular season ending with the #1 seed. However, it was #7 seed Bro. Kelvin Coles that would dominate higher seeds with three commanding 50+ point playoff victories on his way to a 125.68 to 59.06 route of Bro. Andre Harper in the BOS Super Bowl a to capture the championship.

Program Director: Bro. Andre Harper
Committee Members: Bro. C. Hill, Bro. J. McKelvey, Bro. E. Locklear, Bro. C. Marsh, Bro. C. Hopkins, Bro. M. Tyler

What were the intended goals of the program/activity? The goal of the event was to create another way for brothers to interact and stay engaged with chapter activity. We have a 16 team league. The champions wins our BOS "Lombardi" trophy that gets passed to each champion each year.

Type of Media Coverage: Social Media

Brotherhood Event- Cincinnati Bengals Playoffs
Chapter Programming

Date: 1/9/16

Venue/Activity Location: Buffalo Wild Wings
Area of Focus: Membership

Description of Activity/Program: Brotherhood Events provide a relaxed environment where Sigma Brothers can socialize outside of the meetings. Members of BOS met to watch the Cincinnati Bengals take on the Pittsburgh Steelers in the NFL Playoffs.

Program Director: Bro. Andre Harper
Committee Members: Bro. C. Hill, Bro. J. McKelvey, Bro. E. Locklear, Bro. C. Marsh, Bro. C. Hopkins, Bro. M. Tyler

What were the intended goals of the program/activity? The goal of the event was to create another way for brothers to interact and stay engaged with chapter activity.

Community Partners: Zeta Phi Beta Sorority, Inc.
Type of Media Coverage: Social Media

Brotherhood Event- Red, White & Boom
Chapter Programming

Date: 7/1/16

Venue/Activity Location: Downtown Columbus
Area of Focus: Membership

Description of Activity/Program: Brotherhood Events provide a relaxed environment where Sigma Brothers can socialize outside of the meetings. Members of BOS joined over 400,000 people in downtown Columbus to celebrate the 36th annual Red, White & BOOM! This beloved event began in 1981 when 30,000 people gathered in Bicentennial Park to watch a small firework display. The excitement of the downtown Independence Day Celebration has boomed into what is now the largest single day event in Columbus and features the most recognized firework display in the Midwest.

Program Director: Bro. Andre Harper
Committee Members: Bro. C. Hill, Bro. J. McKelvey, Bro. E. Locklear, Bro. C. Marsh, Bro. C. Hopkins, Bro. M. Tyler

What were the intended goals of the program/activity? The goal of the event was to create another way for brothers to interact and stay engaged with chapter activity.

Community Partners: Zeta Phi Beta Sorority, Inc.
Type of Media Coverage: Social Media

2016 Spring Chapter Road Trip
Chapter Programming

Date: 4/1/16 - 4/3/16

Venue/Activity Location: Alpha Eta Chapter Sigma Week (Tallahassee, FL)

Area of Focus: Membership

Description of Activity/Program: The BOS Spring Road Trip provides a relaxed environment where chapter brothers can socialize outside of the meetings by traveling. Members of BOS as well as alumni brothers from Cincinnati, collegiate brothers from the Ohio State University and Bowling Green State University took a road trip to Tallahassee, FL to experience the Sigma Week festivities sponsored by the Alpha Eta Chapter at Florida A&M University. Brothers also stopped in Atlanta to have lunch at Pascal's restaurant that was founded by Bro. James Paschal and his brother Robert.

Program Director: Bro. Andre Harper
Committee Members: Bro. C. Hill, Bro. J. McKelvey, Bro. E. Locklear, Bro. C. Marsh, Bro. C. Hopkins, Bro. M. Tyler

What were the intended goals of the program/activity? The goal of the event was to create another way for brothers to interact and stay engaged with chapter activity.

Type of Media Coverage: Social Media

Chapter Operations

Submitted by: Brother Hiram Jones, President, Beta Omicron Sigma (BOS)

- Chapter operations are good and on an improving trend. The Executive Board has embarked on a journey to improve accountability and member involvement. Strategies and activities to serve the welfare and bonding among members and service in the community has led to enhanced relationships and engagement among members. Communications have also improved greatly and several practices have been instituted to ensure consistent and effective operations.

Chapter Officers include: Derek Lee, First Vice President; James Burke, Second Vice President; Andre Harper, Director of Programs; Joseph McKelvey, Treasurer; Preslin Isaac, Chapter Chaplain; Michael Tyler, Chapter Secretary; Larry Jackson, Director Sigma Beta Club; Rick Henderson, Colligate Advisor

Chapter Budget:

- BOS has a written budget and financial plan for execution. The budget is developed on an annual basis based upon planned and projected revenues and expenditures for the calendar year. Revenue is primarily derived from the payment of local dues by chapter members, donations and proceeds from planned fundraising activities conducted throughout the calendar year.
- The Chapter has established a non-profit, tax exempt foundation to generate charitable contributions to support its Sigma Beta Club Chapter and other community based events.
- A monthly financial report of all accounts' cash receipts and disbursements is provided at each Chapter meeting to provide full transparency and understanding.

Chapter has current and written bylaws

- BOS has a written constitution which governs its structure and operations.

Chapter Conducts Monthly Meetings

- BOS conducts Chapter meetings on the second Saturday of each month at its adopted school South High School, Columbus City Schools, 10:00 AM – 1:00 PM. Chapter officers meet the week prior to each Chapter meeting to coordinate and plan for the session. Chapter members receive notice regarding scheduled meetings and events via email, GroupMe (a group texting application), and the Chapter's calendar which is posted on the Chapter's website and inside the Chapter's Google Docs Drive. During the meetings, attendance is recorded and minutes from the previous meeting are presented and read by the Chapter Secretary. Chapter officers and Committee Chairs provide reports on the progress of their projects and activities. The Robert's Rules of Order is utilized to facilitate parliamentary procedures in conducting chapter business. Interim committee meetings are conducted to support the Chapter's programing objectives. We regularly evaluate our performance against planned goals and objectives as well as the impact that we have in the Central Ohio and surrounding areas.

Chapter has an annual retreat prior to the fall

- BOS conducts a retreat annually to support strategic planning and to set the Chapter's activities and calendar for the coming year. During the retreat a SWOT analysis is performed to review and address both the internal and external environment and to develop strategies and plans to mitigate or eliminate obstacle that might hinder Chapter's operations and objectives. Chapter accomplishments from the previous year are reviewed. Chapter officers, Committee Chairs, and members can engage in discussions regarding contemporary issues and the directions and plans for the chapter. All members are expected to join a committee to facilitation project development activities and an execution plan.

Marketing, Communications, and Social Media:

- The Chapter maintains accounts on Facebook, Twitter, Instagram, and chapter website (www.wearebos.org). All social media content is reviewed by the Communications and Networking Committee and marketing/promotional material is reviewed and approved by the BOS Executive Board prior to posting. All accounts comply with National standards for professionalism and decorum.

Chapter assigned alumni advisor who attends collegiate chapter meetings at least twice a month

- BOS has a Collegiate Affairs committee whose role is to provide oversight, mentoring, and advisory support to the collegiate chapters. Collegiate chapters that fall under the governance of BOS include Delta Omicron (The Ohio State University), Epsilon Omicron (Ohio University), Epsilon Phi (Bowling Green State University) and the collegiate associate members of BOS (comprised of Denison University, Ohio Wesleyan University, Franklin University, Otterbein University, and Capital University).

Campus Advisor attend chapter meeting at least once a month (Collegiate Chapter)

- A member of the Collegiate Affairs committee (including designated advisor) attend Collegiate Chapter meetings and are present at each activity hosted by the collegiate chapter. Reports on the GPAs, projects, programs, membership, and all other necessary information are provided back to the Alumni Chapter for review.

Collegiate officers participate in local alumni Chapter meeting each month

- Collegiate chapters participate in Alumni Chapter meetings as their schedules allow. Increased emphasis is being placed on this requirement to ensure integration and communication.

Chapter supports and participates with local NPHC or other Greek community organizations

- BOS has a primary and secondary liaison who attends monthly NPHC meetings. They share news and programing support requirements during monthly Alumni Chapter meetings. Alumni Chapter President attends quarterly Alumni Chapter President meetings to provide an immediate and empowered voice at the table. BOS supports other National Pan-Hellenic Council organizations through attendance at their respective program, events, and fund raisers.

Chapter has a minimum of 10 members or 20% (Whichever number is smaller) of its membership registered and actively participate in most recent Regional Conference.

- BOS had a total of 10 (27%) members who attended The Great Lakes Regional Conference conducted in Louisville, KY.

Chapter has a minimum of 10 members or 20% (Whichever number is smaller) of its membership registered and actively participate in most recent Conclave.

- BOS had a total of 10 (27%) chapter members who registered and attended Conclave 2015: I Am My Brother's Keeper, located in Little Rock AK.

Risk Management

Members Personal Property

Use of personal property in fraternity activities shall be strictly voluntary and the sole responsibility of the owner. The Phi Beta Sigma Fraternity, Inc. assume no liability or responsibility for any loss or damage to any personal property of members even if used in conjunction with fraternity activities.

Automobiles and Transportation

Phi Beta Sigma Fraternity, Inc. Beta Omicron Sigma Chapter states that any individual who provides transportation in conjunction with fraternity activities does so at their own risk. They are responsible for their own conduct. No member of Phi Beta Sigma Fraternity, Inc. Beta Omicron Sigma Chapter shall be required to provide transportation and any member or Phi Beta Sigma Fraternity, Inc. Beta Omicron Sigma Chapter who provides transportation shall do so only if it is voluntary. Members of Phi Beta Sigma Fraternity, Inc. Beta Omicron Sigma Chapter shall obey all applicable motor vehicle laws, including, but not limited to, those concerning vehicle safety, vehicle operation, financial responsibility and/or insurance, and the transportation and consumption of alcoholic beverages. Operators shall ensure that vehicles are properly maintained, not overloaded, and are operated in a safe manner. Rental vehicles shall be operated in accordance with rental contracts. Use of personal vehicles shall be strictly voluntary and the sole responsibility of the vehicle owner/operator. Financial Responsibility laws generally impose responsibility for accidents on the Driver or Owner of vehicles. The Fraternity assumes no responsibility or liability and provides no insurance to Drivers or Owners of vehicles for accidents or injuries, or for any damages to vehicles not owned by the Fraternity that may be used in conjunction with fraternity activities.

Contractual Agreements and Additional Insured

No chapter, member, or housing organization may enter any written or oral contract or financial agreement using the name of the fraternity. This includes without limitation such agreements as leases, contracts, hold harmless agreements, liability releases, account statements, purchase orders, and hotel or banquet contracts. As the fraternity's insurance, does not afford protections to outside individuals or entities, no chapter, member, or housing organization may enter any written or oral agreement under which the responsibility or liability of some party other than the fraternity is assumed. Additional Insured status under the Fraternity's insurance requires the prior agreement of both the Fraternity and its insurers.

Abusive Behavior

Phi Beta Sigma Fraternity, Inc. Beta Omicron Sigma Chapter have high expectations for the conduct of its members. It is not in conformity with Phi Beta Sigma Fraternity, Inc. expectations that any member or Phi Beta Sigma Fraternity, Inc. Beta Omicron Sigma Chapter would engage in abusive behavior against anyone. Similarly, it is beneath the dignity and standards of Phi Beta Sigma Fraternity, Inc. for any member or Phi Beta Sigma Fraternity, Inc. to engage in fighting. One example of unacceptable, abusive behavior is sexual harassment. Sexual harassment may be directed against a member of either the opposite sex or same sex. It may occur as part of hazing in a group or in a social one-on-one situation. Sexual harassment may include intimidation, bullying or coercion of a sexual nature or the unwelcome and inappropriate promise of rewards such as membership, offices or assignments, in exchange for sexual favors.

Alcohol and Drugs

All chapter facilities and properties in Phi Beta Sigma Fraternity, Inc. Beta Omicron Sigma Chapter shall be alcohol-free at all times and under all circumstances. The implementation of these procedures is a continuation of the ongoing educational efforts of the General Fraternity.

1. The possession, use and/or consumption of any alcoholic beverages by any Fraternity member, Phi Beta Sigma Fraternity, Inc., or guest, during chapter activities, or in any situation sponsored or endorsed by the chapter, must be in compliance with the laws and ordinances of the state, province, city, county, and university/college.
2. No chapter of Phi Beta Sigma Fraternity, Inc. may purchase alcoholic beverages with Fraternity funds, nor may any member or Phi Beta Sigma Fraternity, Inc. in the name of or on behalf of the chapter coordinate the collections of any funds for such a purchase. This includes, but is not limited to, the following: the purchase of kegs, party balls, and other bulk quantities of alcoholic beverages.
3. No chapter of Phi Beta Sigma Fraternity, Inc. may co-sponsor or co-finance a function where alcohol is purchased by any of the host chapters, groups or organizations.
4. The use or distribution of kegs or party balls by the chapter at chapter events is strictly forbidden.
5. The sale of alcoholic beverages by any chapter of Phi Beta Sigma Fraternity, Inc. is strictly forbidden. No chapter of Phi Beta Sigma Fraternity, Inc. shall participate in any activity or action which creates the impression that the chapter is selling alcohol. Examples include, but are not limited to: charging admission to parties, passing the hat, selling empty cups, selling drink tickets, or having vending machines which dispense alcoholic beverages.
6. The use or possession of any unlawful drug in any form is not permitted at any Phi Beta Sigma Fraternity, Inc. function or in any Phi Beta Sigma Fraternity, Inc. chapter facility.
7. Parties and social activities should be open to members, Phi Beta Sigma Fraternity, Inc., and invited guests only. Open parties, meaning those with unrestricted access by nonmembers of the Fraternity, without specific invitation, are prohibited.
8. All undergraduate recruitment functions and recruitment activities associated with or sponsored by any club/association of Phi Beta Sigma Fraternity, Inc. will be alcohol-free.
9. Alcoholic beverages are prohibited at any Phi Beta Sigma Fraternity, Inc. program or initiation ceremony of the chapter.
10. Chapters are strongly encouraged to conduct alcohol and drug awareness programs for members and Phi Beta Sigma Fraternity, Inc.

Hazing

No chapter or member of Phi Beta Sigma Fraternity, Inc. shall indulge in any physical abuse or undignified treatment (hazing). Hazing is defined as: "any action taken or situation created, intentionally or unintentionally, whether on or off Fraternity premises, and whether with or without the consent of the persons subjected to the action, which produces mental or physical discomfort, embarrassment, harassment, or ridicule." Such activities and situations include: paddling in any form, creation of excessive fatigue, physical and psychological shocks, quests, treasure hunts, scavenger hunts, road trips, or any other such activities carried on outside the confines of the chapter facility, wearing apparel in public which is conspicuous and not normally in good taste, engaging in any public stunts and buffoonery, morally degrading or humiliating games and activities, late work sessions which interfere with scholastic activity, and any other activities which are not consistent with fraternal law, ritual, or policy with the regulations and policies of the educational institution.

High-Risk Events

Experience indicates that certain events are of such high risk and the consequences of injuries from engaging in them so devastating that such events are prohibited on Phi Beta Sigma Fraternity, Inc. property or at Phi Beta Sigma Fraternity, Inc. sponsored events. Chapters must take a common-sense approach to evaluating the risk of any events or activities. Should there be any doubt about an activity or event, chapter leaders should contact the Director of Insurance and Safety at Phi Beta Sigma Fraternity, Inc. General Headquarters.

BOS awarded a appreciation award at the Barnett Recreation Center 50th Celebration

Program Implementation Assessments (PIA)

Phi Beta Sigma Fraternity, Inc. has created a standard mechanism for assessment and reporting our national programs and initiatives. Our reporting tool, the electronic Program Implementation Assessment Form captures key result indicators for assessment of key outcomes. These key result indicators (KRI's) are tracked for benchmarking, measuring, and reporting. Incentives and recognition have been created for those chapters who comply and consequences for those chapters who do not complete and submit the PIA Forms.

This tool will capture key result indicators for assessment of the following outcomes:

1. How many people did the program/event reach and/or participate?
2. How many dollars were raised if applicable?
3. What were the goals of the program or activity?
4. Evaluation of program implementation and execution.
5. Number of service hours completed?
6. What was the total expense of project, program or activity?

Report Exported From The Blueprint Submission Database
(as of December 19, 2016)

EVENT DATE	PROGRAM	PROGRAM GOALS	NAT'L PROGRAM	SERVICE HOURS
2/29/2016	The men of the BOS hosted this event at Buckeye Crazy Sports Bar, a minority-owned business as part of Project SEED. We welcomed over 70 family and friends to The Blue Debut: Breaking Blue! We introduced the newest members, Bro. Kabimbi Kalubi and Br	The goal of the event was to promote a local black business, Buckeye Crazy Sports Bar by publicly introduce our newest fraternity to the community. They greeted other members of the Pan-Hellenic Council organizations and did some steps.	Bigger and Better Business	75
4/9/2016	The Sigma Economic Empowerment Development Project (Project SEED) is a Bigger & Better Business program developed to focus on two important topics of interest: Financial Management and Home Ownership. This focus provides useful information in both ar	Soror Tasha Macklin spoke about on Financial and Estate Planning.	Bigger and Better Business	12

11/12/2016	The Beta Omicron Sigma Chapter of Phi Beta Sigma Fraternity, Inc. is hosted our annual Veteran's breakfast, The Blue Salute!	We showed our appreciation of all the sacrifices made by these brave men and women by recognizing them for all they have done to protect the freedom we enjoy.	Bigger and Better Business	105
12/6/2016	The men of the BOS hosted this event at Buckeye Crazy Sports Bar, a minority-owned business as part of Project SEED. We welcomed over 70 family and friends to The Blue Debut: T.U.R.M.O.I.L.E.D Trilogy! We introduced the newest members, Bro. James Smi	This was a joint endeavor to promote the a local black business.	Bigger and Better Business	90
12/13/2016	The Columbus area chapters of Zeta Phi Beta Sorority, Inc. and Phi Beta Sigma Fraternity, Inc. hosted a networking social to collect toys for Columbus area children this holiday season. The toys will be given away at the Breakfast with Sigma Santa Ev	The event is apart of our Bigger and Better Business programmatic thrust because it was held at Buckeye Crazy, a black owned sports bar. We surpassed our goal of collecting over 300 toys.	Bigger and Better Business	90
12/13/2016	The Columbus, OH Area chapters of Zeta Phi Beta Sorority, Inc. (3) and Phi Beta Sigma Fraternity, Inc. (2) held their annual Breakfast with Sigma Santa which provided nearly 300 kids with toys as well as providing breakfast to over 150 parents and vo	We have continued to maintain our presence in the community. We are continuing to establish a tradition of children celebrating the holidays with "Sigma Santa." We set out to provide an opportunity for parents to get information about free tax prepar	Bigger and Better Business	105
9/3/2016	The men of BOS encouraged friends to meet at Buckeye Crazy for the Ohio State University football season opener. We celebrate black owned businesses as part of our Fraternity's Project SEED. The Sigma Economic Empowerment	The is to showcase some of the amazing Black owned businesses in Columbus as well as show off the amazing food and atmosphere of one of the area's great sports bars.	Bigger and Better Business	24

Development Project
(Project

7/25/2016	The Beta Omicron Sigma Chapter presented a $1000 to David Via as part of the chapter's African American Male Leadership Program Scholarship.	The goal of the program is to offer mentoring and scholarships to African-American males.	Education	24
8/20/2016	We held our 11th Annual Blue & White School Supply Drive. Beta Omicron Sigma, along with Zeta Phi Beta Sorority, Inc.-Sigma Iota Zeta Chapter, Reynoldsburg, OH and Zeta Phi Beta Sorority, Inc., Gamma Zeta Zeta Chapter (Columbus, Ohio), collected scho	We collected 4 bins filled with school supplies and over $300 for additional supplies to be distributed to several schools on Columbus's south side.	Education	66
7/17/2016	Each year the SBC and advisors go away on a retreat to prepare for the upcoming school year. Agenda also included building rapport/bonding, a trust building exercise, scavenger hunt, talk about social and life issues, fishing and swimming.	The goals for the event were achieved. Additionally, we explained Robert's Rule of Order, SBC E-board positions and conducted elections. The retreat also included a community service project: cleaned and picked up thrash at the camp.	Sigma Beta Club	120
7/23/2016	The event introduced the newest members of the SBC to the community.	The event introduced the newest members of the SBC to the community.	Sigma Beta Club	12
5/21/2016	Title sponsors for "Breaking the Blues Stigma," hosted by Gamma Zeta Zeta chapter of Zeta Phi Beta Sorority, Inc.	As the title sponsor, we were allotted time to discuss portions of our Living Well Brother-to-Brother initiative, specifically abou black men and the stigmas behind mental health awareness.	Social Action	6

3/1/2016	BOS hosted the Sigma Bazaar where Columbus area families were welcome to get clothing free of charge. We created a welcoming environment with music and brothers assisting with gathering and transporting to vehicles. Guests were encouraged to bring b	Over 250 guests were able to get clothing free of charge at the Sigma Bazaar.	Social Action	160
4/30/2016	BOS is excited about Sigma's leadership role in eliminating health disparities in men of color. Local healthcare professionals gave for screenings and preventative care education. Health care professionals presented information from our health care m	Over 200 guests were able to get free health screening, attend Living Well Brother To Brother sessions lead by local health professionals as well as get information about to access to quality healthcare. Living Well Brother to Brother Modules Complet	Social Action	15
6/2/2016	BOS participated in the The National Gun Violence Awareness Day Event: National Gun Violence Awareness Day (Wear Orange Day). It was created with the goal of pulling the community together to take a unified stand against gun violence. Radio Operation	Members of BOS continue to be active in the Columbus community by engaging in leadership meetings as well as public gatherings to maintain our brand.	Social Action	12
5/1/2016	Phi Beta Sigma partners with the March of Dimes. Through this partnership, the two organizations will work together to prevent premature births and build strong fathers and male role modes in the African American community through sponsoring Strong F	BOS raised $1100, exceeding our chapter goal of $1000. We were joined at the walk by our Sigma Beta Club members, Sorors of Zeta Phi Beta Sorority, Inc., in addition to over 10 chapter members.	Social Action	30

3/26/2016	BOS donated over $250 in Easter egg hunt supplies including baskets, candy and empty eggs for the center's annual youth egg hunt.	BOS has a great relationship with the Barnett Recreation center. The director, Ms. Theresa Featherstone, knows that she can contact BOS and	Social Action	10
	We also donated a $100 Target Gift card for additional supplies.	we will be there to help. She says that we are the only civic organizations that continues to make an ongoing		
8/13/2016	The annual African American Male Wellness Walk Celebrates health & wellness with screenings, Education, Exercise And FUN! 20 Men of BOS participated in the 3 mile walk and 2 brothers ran in the 5 mile run. All brothers participated in health screenin	Over 2000 people enjoyed live entertainment, free health screenings, a 5K walk/run, job fair and free immunizations.	Social Action	60

BOS and Zetas at the 2016 MLK March

Sigma Beta Club

In 1950 Phi Beta Sigma Fraternity became the first Greek organization to develop a youth auxiliary group. Under the direction of Dr. Parlette L. Moore the Sigma Beta Club was founded. Brother Moore was concerned about our changing needs in our communities and recognized the important role that Sigma men could play in the lives of our youth.

The Sigma Beta Clubs' four major principles of focus are on Culture, Athletics, Social and Educational needs. The Sigma Beta Club offers a unique opportunity to develop values, leadership skills and social/cultural awareness in our youth during their developmental years. Sigma Beta Club programs are geared to meet the needs of its members, but at the same time provide them with a well-rounded outlook that is needed to cope with today's society. Phi Beta Sigma is confident that investing in our youth today will produce the effective leaders of tomorrow.

The Sigma Beta Club sponsored by Beta Omicron Sigma Chapter is directed by Bro. Larry Jackson, Hon. Bro. Carter D. Womack, Bro. Preslin Isaac, Bro. Joseph Copeland, Bro. John Merriweather & Bro. John Jackson. It is based out of Columbus South High School. It is officially charted by the International Headquarters. Its members meet regularly throughout the school year. In addition to meetings they are very involved in school activities, community service with the fraternity as well as their own events, self-enrichment and social activities.

Sigma Beta Club
Annual Retreat

Date: July 17-19, 2016

Venue/Activity Location: Grange Friendly Hills Campsite (Zanesville, Ohio)
Area of Focus: Sigma Beta Club

Description of Activity/Program: Each year the SBC and advisors go away on a retreat to prepare for the upcoming school year. Agenda also included building rapport/bonding, a trust building exercise, scavenger hunt, talk about social and life issues, fishing and swimming.

Program Chair: Bro. Larry Jackson
Committee Members: Hon. Bro. Carter D. Womack Bro. Preslin Isaac, Bro. Joseph Copeland, Bro. John Merriweather & Bro. John Jackson

What were the intended goals of the program/Activity: The goals for the event were achieved. Additionally, we explained Robert's Rule of Order, SBC Eboard positions and conducted elections. The retreat also included a community service project: cleaned and picked up thrash at the camp.

Number of Service Hours: 120
Number of people served: 14

Type of Media Coverage: Social Media

Sigma Beta Club
Car Wash

Date: July 23, 2016

Venue/Activity Location: O'Reilly Auto Parts
Area of Focus: Fundraising

Description of Activity/Program: Each year the SBC and advisors go away on a retreat to prepare for the upcoming school year. Agenda also included building rapport/bonding, a trust building exercise, scavenger hunt, talk about social and life issues, fishing and swimming.

Program Chair: Bro. Larry Jackson
Committee Members: Hon. Bro. Carter D. Womack Bro. Preslin Isaac, Bro. Joseph Copeland, Bro. John Merriweather & Bro. John Jackson

What were the intended goals of the program/Activity: The event was a fundraiser for upcoming programs and events.

Number of Service Hours: 6
Number of people served: 14

Type of Media Coverage: Social Media

**2016 Annual Chapter Report
BETA OMICRION SIGMA CHAPTER
Columbus, OH
www.WeAreBOS.org**

Sigma Beta Club
SBC Induction Ceremony

Date: July 23, 2016

Venue/Activity Location: South High School
Area of Focus: Membership

Description of Activity/Program: The event introduced the newest members of the SBC to the community.

Program Chair: Bro. Larry Jackson
Committee Members: Hon. Bro. Carter D. Womack Bro. Preslin Isaac, Bro. Joseph Copeland, Bro. John Merriweather & Bro. John Jackson

What were the intended goals of the program/Activity: The event introduced the newest members of the SBC to the community.

Number of Service Hours: 12
Number of people served: 14

Type of Media Coverage: Social Media

Sigma Beta Club
Rise and Thunder Curriculum

Date: October 20, 2016

Venue/Activity Location: Rocky Fork Metro Parks Haunted Hike

Description of Activity/Program: Two Sigma Beta Club members along with three chapter advisors participated in the Rocky Fork Metro Parks Annual Hunted Hike. This activity falls within the scope of the Sigma Beta Club Rise and Thunder Curriculum along with the Fraternity's Childhood Obesity & Health and Wellness Initiative.

Program Chair: Bro. L. Jackson
Committee Members: Bro. H. Jones and Bro. J. Jackson

What were the intended goals of the program/Activity: The Beta's helped support a local organization called Handshake Columbus, which is a student organization in the Central Ohio area that pairs up with leaders in the community to serve as mentors for high school students by showing them mutual appreciation and life lesson learned through athletic competition, while teaching future generations about what a handshake might reveal about a person's character on and off the field.

Number of Service Hours: 15
Number of People: 5

Community Partners: Columbus South High School 7-12, Canal Winchester High
Type of Media Coverage: Social Media, School Yearbook and School Newspaper.

Sigma Beta Club
Rise and Thunder Curriculum

Date: December 21, 2016

Venue/Activity Location: Wayne Webb's Bowling Lane

Description of Activity/Program: Four Sigma Beta Club members along with six chapter advisors participated in the Beta's annual Christmas bowling party. This activity falls within the scope of the Sigma Beta Club Rise and Thunder Curriculum along with the Fraternity's Childhood Obesity & Health and Wellness Initiative.

Program Chair: Bro. L. Jackson
Committee Members: Bro. P. Isaac, Bro. J. Merriweather, Bro. J. Jackson, Bro. J. Copeland and Bro. W. Damson

What were the intended goals of the program/Activity: This is the Sigma Beta Club's annual Christmas celebration. The Betas fellowshipped with current and past SBC members as well as their advisors. They earned service hours for mentoring. They fulfilled requirements for the Rise and Thunder Curriculum.

Number of Service Hours: 18
Number of People: 10

Community Partners: Columbus South High School 7-12, Canal Winchester High School and The Charles School
Type of Media Coverage: Social Media, School Yearbook and School Newspaper.

Media Relations

Overview

The Media Relations Committee went through a structural renaissance in 2016. As a committee, we identified the need for more effective publicizing and marketing of all chapter activities. The committee's purpose is to provide effective marketing strategies for all chapter functions. Also, the functions of the Media Relations Chair shifted to become to the channel of communications for media-related business. This was a radical change brought forth to ensure that the chapter's voice within the community can remain as one.

Accomplishments

Full Establishment of Media Relations Director Position

The Media Relations Chair position was created, in part, to give the chapter a publicity, marketing, and branding direction. Prior to the creation of the position, the Correspondence Secretary handled all the social media, brand, and marketing responsibilities. With the growth of social media and digital branding, this task seemed daunting for one person to handle and could prove a hindrance in future administrations. With the official establishment of the Media Relations Chair, a new Executive Board position was established for Beta Omicron Sigma. In short, the Media Relations Chair oversees the following 5 areas of the chapter:

- Public Relations
- Branding
- Marketing
- Social Media (Digital Life) Management
- Website Management

With one person focusing on these areas, the various committees within the chapter can now divert their focus primarily on planning and implementation of goals set forth by the Chapter President. This will also give a point-of-contact for events, as well as a spokesperson to speak on behalf of the chapter to media and media-related outlets. The Media Relations Chair does not work autonomously, but as the voice of the chapter and its executive board. The positon is an appointed position with no term limits nor designated time of appointment.

Social Media

One of the social media goals is to increase public participation. While we are still tabulating our increased website traffic, we saw another year of drastic increase via Facebook. We started the year at 397 Likes and we ended the year at 533 Likes, an increase of 136. This jump was due to our continued commitment to post a variety of events, but not solely relying on pictures and video, but using Facebook Live and other sources of technology. It is the committee's wish to continue our increase on Facebook, as well as shift our focus on other social media platforms, such as Instagram and LinkedIn. We will continue to operate our Twitter account, however due to its functionality, we have found this has been the least effective manner of transmitting information to the demographics we desire to hit.

Media Relations

We have continued to established relationships with different media groups within the Columbus area. Our events have been mentioned on WBNS-TV's Community Calendar. We have also been featured multiples times in the Fraternity Weekly Newsletter. We look to start a relationship with radio and niche communication platforms to continue our reach throughout Columbus.

Branding

We have continued to update our branding to not only be universal in look, but to match the Fraternity branding standards that we are required to meet. Through 2016, we have updated our digital system so that all committee and general members who present information are using the Fraternity's PowerPoint template. We have also established the branding for our chapter seal. Our chapter seal is used for brother-only documents and correspondences. All other documents will now have the international seal.

The chapter seal was a collaborative design effort brought by Bros. Michael Tyler II & L'Nard Tufts II. General members gave input on the first concept and the Media Relations team went forth and completed the design.

Public Relations

We established a channel of communication in the event the media would like to establish a line of communication with the chapter. We also served as a title sponsor for the Mental Health Awareness event, hosted by Zeta Phi Beta Sorority, Inc., Gamma Zeta Zeta chapter. This gave us a prime location within the event to display our accomplishments and were featured on a radio spot promoting the event. In addition, myself and Bro. Lohit Solomon gave brief remarks on the state of mental health, from the perspective of African-American men.

Submitted By: Bro. Michael Tyler II, Chapter Secretary & Director of Media Relations

Committee Members: Bro. John Jackson, Bro. Richard Taylor, Bro. L'Nard Tufts II

Additional 2016 Chapter Programming

What Of The Day Movie Premier
Chapter Programming

Date: 2/6/16

Venue/Activity Location: Pan African Film Festival in Los Angeles at Rave Cinemas-Baldwin Hills
Area of Focus: Fraternity Special Event

Description of Activity/Program: Bro. Andre Harper traveled to Los Angeles, CA. to represent BOS at the world premier of *What Of The Day*. The documentary movie was commissioned and produced by Jonathan A. Mason, Sr., International President and the General Board of Phi Beta Sigma Fraternity Inc., in association with With Grace Productions and written and directed by Brother Anthony A. Samad, Ph.D., the film tells the story of the significance of the black fraternity movement in America, and chronicles Phi Beta Sigma Fraternity, Inc. activities, as it prepared to celebrate its 100th Anniversary.

Program Director: Bro. Andre Harper
Committee Members: Bro. C. Hill, Bro. J. McKelvey, Bro. E. Locklear, Bro. C. Marsh, Bro. C. Hopkins, Bro. M. Tyler

What were the intended goals of the program/activity? The goal of the event was to make sure that BOS had representation at this historic event.

Type of Media Coverage: Social Media

For The Lover In You
Chapter Programming

Date: 2/9/16

Venue/Activity Location: Ruth's Chris Steak House
Area of Focus: Fundraising

Description of Activity/Program: BOS hosted "For The Lover In You, " Valentine's Day themed Happy Hour and Charity Raffle to raise money for chapter operations and programming. The event was held at the upscale Ruth Chris Steakhouse where guests were treated to drink specials and complimentary appetizers. The grand prize winner of "The Blue Escape," won a $200 Ruth Chris Dinner, One (1) Night Hotel Stay, Blue "Beats By Dre" Pill (for your midnight soundtrack) & A Bottle of Wine.

Program Director: Bro. Andre Harper
Committee Members: Bro. C. Hill, Bro. J. McKelvey, Bro. E. Locklear, Bro. C. Marsh, Bro. C. Hopkins, Bro. M. Tyler

What were the intended goals of the program/activity? The goal of the event was to raise money for chapter operations and programming. The event was well attended and the chapter made a profit.

Number of Service Hours: 99
Number of people served? 30
Type of Media Coverage: Social Media, PBS- Weekly News

Conclave 2015: I Am My Brother's Keeper
Little Rock, AK

2016 Great Lakes Regional Conference
Louisville, KY

GREAT LAKES
Φ Β Σ
2016 REGIONAL CONFERENCE
LOUISVILLE
KENTUCKY

The Great Lakes Regional conference was held in Louisville, KY at the prestigious Galt House. BOS several BOS members were attendance. Zeta Phi Beta Sorority, Inc. had their regional conference at the same hotel.

2016 Serious Sigma Summit
Orlando, Florida

As we proceed into "The Next 100 Years" Phi Beta Sigma Fraternity, Inc. held the 2016 Serious Sigma Summit in Orlando, Florida. It provided members a unique opportunity to gain training in leadership, chapter, and personal development. Our international leaders and Sigma Leadership Academy planned an exciting agenda featuring three tracks of focused workshops and seminars, as well as a Collegiate Advisors University. Activities included the Barbershop: "Looking Towards the Next 100", The Sigma Museum, The Serious Sigma Summit Dinner: A Salute to Honorable Dr. Gilbert Francis & Soror Edith V. Francis, a Greek Step Show and Hip Hop Concert.

BOS brothers made the trip to Orlando to be a part of the summit. BOS chapter brother, Honorable Carter D. Womack, was making an impact as part of the fraternity leadership and event organizers.

National Pan-Hellenic Council, Columbus Alumni Chapter

The National Pan-Hellenic Council, Incorporated (NPHC) is currently composed of nine (9) International Greek letter Sororities and Fraternities: Alpha Kappa Alpha Sorority, Inc. Alpha Phi Alpha Fraternity, Inc., Delta Sigma Theta Sorority, Inc., Zeta Phi Beta Sorority, Inc., Iota Phi Theta Fraternity, Inc., Kappa Alpha Psi Fraternity, Inc., Sigma Gamma Rho Sorority, Inc. Phi Beta Sigma Fraternity, Inc. and Omega Psi Phi Fraternity, Inc. NPHC promotes interaction through forums, meetings and other mediums for the exchange of information and engages in cooperative programming and initiatives through various activities and functions.

National Pan-Hellenic Council, Columbus Alumni Chapter ## **2016 NPHC Council Retreat**

Date: 8/14/16

Venue/Activity Location: The Berwick Manor
Area of Focus: National Pan-Hellenic Council

Description of Activity/Program: The men of BOS participated in the annual NPHC retreat to discuss the mission and activities for the 2017 programming year. BOS sent 3 delegates.

Pan-Hellenic Council Representative: Bro. C. Hill
Committee Members: Bro. Hiram Jones, Bro. Ulysses Ford and Bro. James Burke

What were the intended goals of the program/activity To continue our participation and leadership in the local council.

Community Partners: National Pan-Hellenic Council, Columbus Alumni Chapter

Type of Media Coverage: Social Media

National Pan-Hellenic Council, Columbus Alumni Chapter
2nd Annual Black and White Gala Awards Ceremony

Date: 6/24/16

Venue/Activity Location: The Berwick Manor

Area of Focus: National Pan-Hellenic Council

Description of Activity/Program: BOS was a contributing chapter to the National Pan-Hellenic Council, Columbus Alumni Chapter's Biennial Gala. The event celebrates the service & achievements of the Black Greek Letter Organizations in the Greater Columbus Community. Beta Omicron Sigma took home some hardware at the 2nd annual NPHC of Columbus Black and White Gala Awards Ceremony. The chapter received the Outstanding Service Award for Health, in recognition of the Sigma Bazaar. Also, Bro. Michael Tyler II won the Professional Achievement Award for Education & Training, for his work in Black History and Civil Rights Education.

Pan-Hellenic Council Representative: Bro. C. Hill
Committee Members: Bro. Hiram Jones, Bro. Ulysses Ford and Bro. James Burke

What were the intended goals of the program/activity?

Community Partners: National Pan-Hellenic Council, Columbus Alumni Chapter

Type of Media Coverage: Social Media

National Pan-Hellenic Council, Columbus Alumni Chapter
2016 NPHC Unity Weekend Cookout

Date: 6/25/16

Venue/Activity Location: Big Walnut Park

Area of Focus: National Pan-Hellenic Council

Description of Activity/Program: BOS was a contributing chapter to the National Pan-Hellenic Council, Columbus Alumni Chapter's 2016 NPHC Unity Weekend Cookout.

Pan-Hellenic Council Representative: Bro. C. Hill
Committee Members: Bro. Hiram Jones, Bro. Ulysses Ford and Bro. James Burke

What were the intended goals of the program/activity?

Community Partners: National Pan-Hellenic Council, Columbus Alumni Chapter

Type of Media Coverage: Social Media

BOS In The News

Φ Β Σ WEEKLY *Update*

February 18, 2016

BETA OMICRON SIGMA HOST "FOR THE LOVER IN YOU" FOR VALENTINES DAY

The Beta Omicron Sigma Chapter (Columbus, OH) hosted the 2016 "For the Lover in You". Guests enjoyed great food and conversation. The grand prize winner received A night at The Marriott, a $200 Gift card at Ruth's Chris, bottle of wine and a Beats by Dre Pill ($200 value) to celebrate Valentines Day.

May 12, 2016

BETA OMICRON SIGMA HOST ANNUAL SIGMA BAZAAR & HEALTH FAIR

The brothers of the Beta Omicron Sigma Chapter, Columbus, OH, held their annual Sigma Bazaar & Health Fair in Columbus, OH at the Barnett Recreation Center. The chapter gave away clothing to two hundred families in need. Thousands of clothing items were donated to the cause. Local healthcare professionals were available for screenings and preventative care education.

August 25, 2016

BETA OMICRON SIGMA PARTICIPATES IN THE AFRICAN AMERICAN MALE WELLNESS WALK

The Beta Omicron Sigma Chapter (Columbus, OH) participated in the annual African American Male Wellness Walk. Over 2000 people enjoyed live entertainment, free health screenings, a 5K walk/run, job fair and free immunizations. 20 Men of BOS and the Sigma Beta Club participated in the 3 mile walk and 2 brothers completed the 5 mile run. All brothers participated in health screenings including blood pressure, blood, body mass and HIV testing.

December 29, 2016

COLUMBUS, OH BLUE AND WHITE HOST ANNUAL BREAKFAST WITH SIGMA SANTA

The Columbus, OH Area chapters of Zeta Phi Beta Sorority, Inc. and Phi Beta Sigma Fraternity, Inc. held their annual Breakfast with Sigma Santa which provided nearly 300 kids with toys as well as providing breakfast to over 150 parents and volunteers. They presented the Barnett Recreation Center a $300 check for center programs. Kids had their pictures taken with Sigma Santa and parents received information about free tax preparation through the Volunteer Income Tax Assistance (VITA) from volunteer financial advisers. Parents were also able to meet with representatives from Federal Express were on hand to hire new employees.

2016 Annual Chapter Report
BETA OMICRION SIGMA CHAPTER
Columbus, OH
www.WeAreBOS.org

BOS 2016 Event Gallery

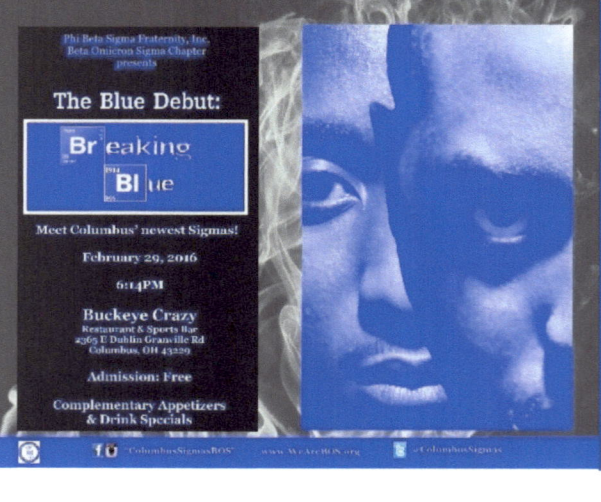

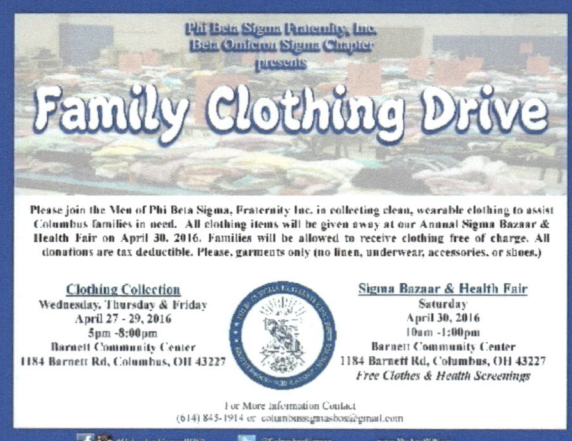

2016 Annual Chapter Report
BETA OMICRION SIGMA CHAPTER
Columbus, OH
www.WeAreBOS.org

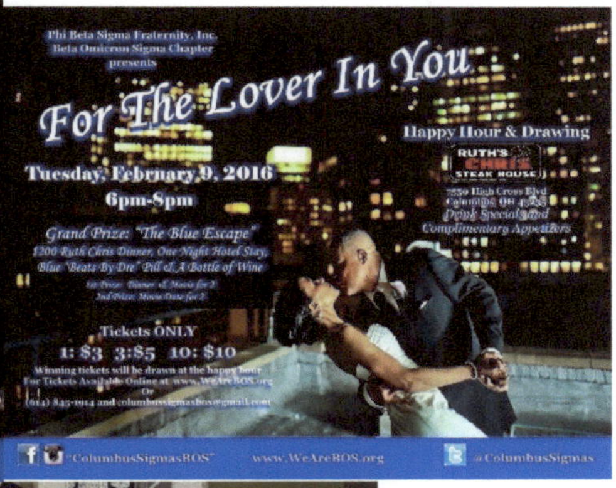

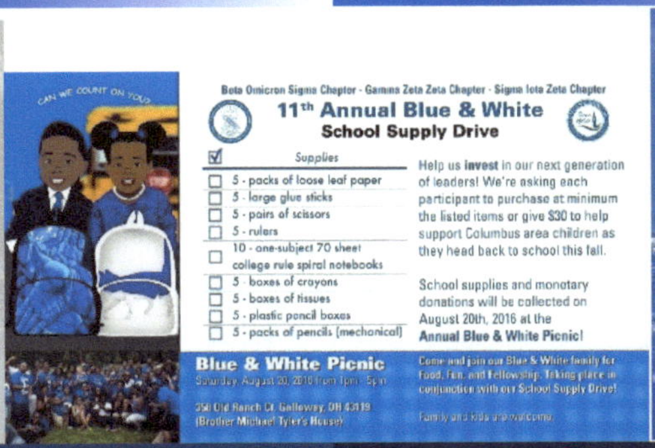